MW00975887

The Promise Is Mine

God's Faithfulness through Broken

Relationships

Copyright © 2015 by Loretta Davis. All rights reserved and no portion of this publication may be reproduced, stored in a retrieval system, or transmitted in any form by any means— electronic, mechanical, photocopying, recording, or any other—except for brief quotations in printed reviews, without the prior written permission of the publisher Scripture quotations are from the New King James Version of the Bible.

Library of Congress Cataloging-in-Publication Data - Loretta Davis

Cover Designed by Bevcottondesign@com

Table of Content

For the vision is yet for an appointed time, but at the end it shall speak, and not lie: though it tarry, wait for it; because it will surely come, it will not tarry.

Habakkukk 2:3

Dedication

This book is dedicated to the Lord Jesus Christ who is the Lord of my life. His love is the true author of this book. I am only a vessel whom He has chosen to go "through the furnace of affliction" to reveal His will, purpose, and plan for my life. Throughout this book you will find God's love, long suffering, faithfulness, and His grace and mercy.

I also dedicate this book to my precious children: Telly, Katrice, Marcus, and Jared. They were the drafted soldiers who withstood the storm and are witnesses that this story is true. This book is dedicated to those who are in some type of bondage and who think they have no way out. I pray that after you read this book you will come to realize that there are alternatives. The first alternative is making Jesus the Lord of your life and then letting Him fulfill the purpose and the plan that He has for your life. Then He will bring you into your divine destiny, which He has created for you since before the foundation of this world.

No matter what storm you are facing, or will go through, He is able to carry you, if you totally let Him have His way. The outcome may not be the way you think, but if you trust the Lord, He will do what's best for you. Remember, He said in His Word, "For my thoughts are not your thoughts, neither are your ways my ways, saith the Lord", (Isaiah 55:8).

Why don't you just stop right now and ask God to have His "way" in whatever situation you are experiencing. When the Lord gives you a promise concerning your situation, hold onto it and let go of the "apparent circumstances". Then you will see the faithfulness of God, and He will surely bring joy.

For my thoughts are not your thoughts, neither are your ways my ways, saith the Lord.

(Isaiah 55:8)

Acknowledgments

I would like to thank the Lord Jesus Christ, and the Father, for taking that which the devil meant for bad, and turning it to good. I realize that I am only a vessel chosen by God to reveal Him through my testimony. I acknowledge that it was He who was carrying me every step of the way. It was His grace and mercy that picked me up and His love that sustained me. If I had not gone through this situation, I would have been unable to write this book. All praise and honor to God!

Special thanks go to my family for praying for me and believing in me when it seemed impossible for any good thing to happen. I know that there were times when my family's heart ached to see my children and I go through such suffering, but took what the devil means for evil and turned it to a blessing.

Thanks to my children whom I love so dearly and who is one of my greatest supporters. They are the walls that God used to hold me up, push me forward, and bring me forth.

A special blessing to my mother, Murphy Reid, who was the vessel God used to plant this seed of hope into my life.

In the midst of my trials my mother said, "Loretta, one day you might write a book." At that very moment, I became "Pregnant" with a promise. This "baby" was nurtured through prayer, fed with faith, and sustained through obedience.

Much gratitude to my former pastors, Rev. David and Frances Allen of First Assembly of God in Natchitoches, Louisiana. They were the co-captains in the ship that kept me on course when the storm began to rage in my life. They sounded the alarm with the un-compromised Word of God by saying, "Don't jump ship! There is light at the end of the tunnel". I would like to acknowledge several other special people who were a great influence in my life that were part of helping me bring this book to its final completion.

A very special honor goes to Bishop T.D. Jakes and First Lady Sarita Jakes. Bishop Jakes was the person whom the Lord used to speak a word to my heart in due season which helped pull me from the storm that had been raging in my life for many years. I would like to thank you, Bishop Jakes, for obeying the Lord when you preached the message "A Satisfied Woman". I had never seen you, or heard of you, and the Lord placed one of your tapes in my hands when it was time for my deliverance. I was the woman who was living in an abusive relationship and felt trapped because I thought I had no alternatives. When you spoke those anointed words, "With God on your side you can do anything", it broke through the bars of my prison cell and God was able to pull me out.

Thank you for your ministry that has helped so many people.

I would like to thank Pastor Benny and Mrs. Suzanne Hinn with whom the Lord divinely connected me with to help to serve in their ministry for six and a half years. I would like to thank them for this privilege and for helping and allowing me to fulfill the call God placed upon my life. The Lord allowed me to serve in their ministry to prepare me for greater responsibilities.

A special appreciation goes to my editors Mr. Gregg Oreo and Mr. Anthony Gardner. Mr. Oreo said something that encouraged me, "Many people are called to write a book, but few complete it".

A special gratitude to J. Don George, of Calvary Church. Pastor George recognized the calling of God on my life and encouraged me to go forward when I was wavering. The Lord used Pastor George to confirm that calling to me. The night a professional singer "Stacy Michael" was in concert at our church, she stated that God was preparing someone for ministry who is sitting in the service.

I said, "Lord, if you're talking to me, confirm it". Then she gave an altar call, and I went up along with others. Pastor George walked up to me and said, "Loretta, you know God is talking to you, and I have come to confirm it, and I release you to go out and minister, and I pray that the anointing never leaves you".

A very special appreciation goes to Ms. Vickie Goble who helped me to start the process of putting the book together by allowing me to use her computer to type the manuscript.

Also, thanks to Mr. David Carpenter. After several years of pondering, and asking the Lord what to name this book, the confirmation came when I shared my testimony with David. He said, "You need to write a book and you need to name it <u>The Promise is Mine</u>". Immediately, I felt a witness in my spirit! I felt something leap within me saying, "This is it"! This was the season I began to write all that the Lord had deposited in me.

A Word from My Parents

Loretta is a person who really loves the Lord with all of her heart. We believe, as you read her book, you will be blessed tremendously.

When Loretta changed her denomination (from the one she was raised in) and received the baptism of the Holy Spirit, we noticed a big change in her life. She started living differently, not just by going to church regularly but also by loving the Lord more devotedly. We witnessed how the Lord brought her through many storms and how He used them to bring her closer to Him. In praying, and standing with Loretta, the Lord allowed us to see Him at work in her.

We witnessed many miracles that she encountered while she walked with the Lord. He had done miracles in our lives but there was something different about the way Loretta gave God glory before her answers came. She would stand on God's Word and have full assurance that God had already done His divine work.

When she shared with us about how God showed her a vision of her sitting in His hand and how He carried her through the storm with a rainbow at the end, we knew there was a grand promise in store. It was then we felt that one day Loretta would write a book as a way of sharing these great testimonies with others.

Loretta can hold people in suspense for hours by recalling the miracles God has done in her life. They leave in awe, wanting to experience miracles in their lives too. As you read her book you can witness the miracles, along with the tribulations, that she experienced which revealed the glory of God. We believe the Lord will allow her to share in her next book about the supernatural miracles that she encountered while riding through the storms with Jesus.

When Loretta moved to Dallas, we felt this was a new beginning for her ministry. Our prayer is that when you read "The Promise Is Mine", you will be so moved that you'll allow God to move your faith to another level. God bless you, "Highly Favored One"!

A Word from My Daughter

My mother is truly a blessing to me! Because of the struggles we have faced as a family I have become a stronger person, mother, wife, and a young woman of God. The Lord has always taken care of my family even through the most difficult times. I will always remember to call on the Lord for anything I need. My mom has taught me that Jesus is the Way, the Truth, and the Life and that through God, ALL THINGS ARE POSSIBLE!

I Love you mom and may God bless you!

Katrice Baker Below

Introduction

When the Lord gave me this assignment, in the year 2000, to write a book, I couldn't imagine where to begin. I said "Lord, "I don't know how to even start it, and I don't have 'one dime' to get it published"! The Lord said to me, "If you're concerned about not having the resources to publish before you write then you won't write the book". As I attempted to start writing, I got a little frustrated because I didn't know how to take all that God had put inside of me and put it into a book.

Then I begin to allow doubt to enter my mind, which made me think that God had not even spoken to me about this. I began to feel that I did not have the ability to perform this task because it seemed too big for me. Then the Lord reminded me of the men and women whom He used in the Bible. None of them could accomplish the task He gave them to do by their own strength or abilities. It was through the Lord's supernatural power that He gave them that enable them to accomplish the things they did. This brought courage to my heart and made me even more willing to obey God.

Later that afternoon, I felt led to attend the evening service. I had a feeling that the Lord had a special message for me. The Pastor's son-in-law was ministering in the service that night. In the beginning of his message he said something that caught my attention.

He said, "I know some of you might recall my sermon of two months ago entitled, 'From Infinity to Beyond,' this evening I'm going to preach part two." He went on to say, "God gave Moses an assignment to bring the children of Israel out of Egypt." He said, "Like God may have given you an assignment to write a book, and you may not know how to get started, but tonight I'm going to tell you how to get started!" I knew that this was God speaking to me and giving me a boost in order to start the process.

I didn't feel qualified to do the job but God assured me that if He calls me, He will qualify me. All He was asking me to do was to be a willing-and-obedient vessel for His use.

That brought comfort to my heart because I knew that He was going to manifest it through me. The Lord gave me everything I needed to accomplish the task; a computer, divine connection, and people to encourage me when I began to procrastinate. He also gave me His Word when I began to grow weary.

The Promise Is Mine

When I grew weary I said, "Lord, I'm tired and I need a word from you that I'm doing what you have told me to do." Then I open my Bible and it fell open to II Chronicles 15:7 which says, "Be ye strong therefore, and let not your hands be weak: for your work shall be rewarded." (II Chronicles 15:7). What an encouraging word I received from the Lord! It was what I needed and when I needed it.

I want to encourage those to whom the Lord has given a special assignment or calling. First admit to Him that you can't do it, but He can! Then He will strengthen you for the task so He can accomplish His purpose through your obedience. When the Lord asks you to do something, He is asking for you to let Him display His ability through you! Do you have something that God is asking for and your disobedience won't allow you to release it? What is He asking you for that already belong to Him? Is He asking you to write a book to display His glory? Is He calling you to preach the Gospel in a much bigger way, that will require you to depend on Him and Him alone? Are you hiding behind someone else calling when God has called you to the forefront? Sometimes it seems much easier to stay back in the shadows where you don't have to use your faith or find yourself totally depending on Him. Give the Lord back what is already His "property" and you'll get to see His glory unfold. And remember: He shares His eminence with no one!

I have no doubt that the Lord has ordered my steps in writing this book. I pray that your life will be touched in a special way upon reading it.

I felt the Lord wanted me to be very "transparent" so people who are in similar circumstances or situations could receive their personal deliverance. Also, they will come to know Him in an intimate way. My desire is that God will be glorified and the reader changed.   Remember that God is no respecter of persons; the same thing He did for me; He will do for you! If you get a little uncomfortable in reading this book, perhaps it's not for you, but for someone you know who needs God's mercy. Please don't hesitate to pass The Promise Is Mine on to someone in need, because people are dying in their sins every day, and every minute, and the Lord wishes no person to perish, but for all to come to repentance. May God richly bless you and may you fulfill your destiny. Remember, the promise can be yours too!

About the Author

Loretta Davis is from Natchitoches, Louisiana. She is the third of six children. Loretta has four sisters (Loleatta, Doretha, Altonette, Sonya) and one brother (Morris Reid, Jr.). Ms. Davis is proud to be the daughter of Morris and Murphy Reid and the granddaughter of the late Mary Lee Payne. She has four children (Telly, Katrice, Marcus, and Jarred) and seven grandchildren (Sayla, Caleb, Isaiah, Breana, Jaylan, Jarrell, Brooke and Morgan).

Loretta was "born again" at the age of twelve at First Baptist Church-Amulet in her hometown (Natchitoches, Louisiana).

Later, in here young parenting years, her hardships and pain led her to find a personal relationship with the Lord Jesus Christ. She was filled with the Holy Spirit at the First Assembly of God Church, which is now known at Oasis of Love Fellowship, where David and Frances Allen serves as pastors. She served as an active member in the choir and women's ministry for fifteen years.

In 1985, she began to feel the call of God upon her life. The Lord confirmed this calling at an altar one night. The Pastor said to her, "I feel God has a calling on your life," but you're not to run off and leave your family, because your ministry can wait until your children are grown." At that moment, she determined in her heart to bring them up in the love, fear, and admonition of the Lord, according to His Word.

There was a time in her life when she found herself in a situation that she thought she had no way out. Loretta married unequally yoked, and because of his addiction to alcohol, there was heartbreak and pain in our family. These trials drove her to her knees to seek the Lord with all of her heart because she knew only God could deliver her. One night, in a vision, she saw herself sitting in God's hand and His hand was moving slowly through a storm. At the end of the storm He revealed the most beautiful rainbow to her. Then He dropped a promise in her heart by saying, "This night have I promise to bring you deliverance".

Shortly after the vision, the Lord woke her up and said to her, "Get up and write the vision down". As she began to write she said, "Lord, what does the rainbow represent"? The Lord said, "It's a Covenant; promise; this night have I promise to bring you deliverance". She placed her hand over her heart because the words burned so deeply.

The next day, the Lord confirmed those words to her during the Sunday morning service. As the Pastor began preaching, he held his Bible up and said, "The Holy Ghost gave me a message to preach this morning: Great Deliverance Giveth He to His Anointed." He went on to say, "The Lord may have dropped a promise into your heart during the night, but that's not to say you're not going to have to go through the storm, but the promise will bring you to the other side"!

Then he began to speak from the book of Acts about God sending an angel-delivered message to Paul during the storm. It reads: "And now I exhort you to be of good cheer: for there shall be no loss of any man's life among you, but of the ship. For there stood by me this night the angel of God, whose I am, and whom I serve, Saying, Fear not, Paul; thou must be brought before Caesar: and, lo, God hath given thee all them that sail with thee. Wherefore, sirs, be of good cheer: for I believe God that it shall be even as it was told me" (Acts 27:22-25). Because of the promise Paul had received from the angel, he could encourage those on the ship that they were going to make it through the stormy seas.

The Lord did not take Loretta out of the situation she was in; He carried her through it. He knew that this trial would bring her closer to Him and help her to surrender to His will for her life.

Loretta was in bondage to this situation for <u>thirteen years</u>, but God's grace and mercy brought her through! The Lord gave her the promise as an anchor that holds the ship during the storm to help bring her through.

The Lord taught her, through this trial, how to believe in Him, trust Him, and wait on Him. He revealed Himself to her in so many ways. He revealed His unconditional love when He allowed His grace and mercy to carry her. His provision stepped in when it seemed all hope was gone! As she began to dwell in His "secret place," through prayer, His presence was her protection.

In the book of Habakkuk 2:3, the Lord says: "For the vision is yet for an appointed time, but at the end it shall speak, and not lie: though it tarry, wait for it; because it will surely come it will not tarry" (Hab. 2:3). That means, God has set a particular time for it to happen, and it will surely happen in God's timing!

If you are in the midst of a storm in your life, begin to seek the Lord and let Him give you a promise concerning that situation. Then hold onto the promise because it will surely come to pass. It states in the book of Numbers: "God is not a man, that he should lie; nor the son of man, that he should repent: has he said, shall he not do it? Or hath he spoken, and shall he not make it good?" (Numbers. 23:19).

During all the years Loretta was hurting and crying out to the Lord, she could not fathom the plans He had in store for her. As she trusted him to lead her, His plans began to unfold in ways that she would never have dreamed. He has allowed her to walk through doors that only He could open.

The Lord has graced Loretta with a special anointing to sing by the power of the Holy Ghost. This anointing was a blanket that swaddled her brokenness. Then the Lord took her pain, tears, and disappointments and turned them into precious "oil". This is what she now holds in the "alabaster box." Each time she presents this alabaster box to Jesus, He unlocks it and pour onto many lives. Through her brokenness and shame many are healed, delivered, and made whole. The gifts and talents that God has entrusted to her have truly brought her before great men of God.

Loretta Davis is now the founder of Heart Changing Ministries, CEO of New Life Publishing, Inspirational Speaker, and a former Television talk show host of "Enjoying the Married Life" program.

My Salvation Experience

The need for a Savior came to me during a revival service at the age of twelve. My parents attended First Baptist Church in Natchitoches, Louisiana, where the late Rev. H. B. Barnum served as pastor. We attended every weekly service, including revivals.

The traditions, in those days, were communions every fourth Sunday, prayer meetings on Wednesday, and revival services every summer.

A revival service was held for two weeks for those who wanted to pray for their "religion." If you were one of those seeking your religion, you would sit in the front on what they would call a "mourner's bench" during the service. Each night, before the revival service was over, the pastor would extend his hand and ask anyone to come forward if they wanted to join the church. If you felt you had "received your religion" during the revival services, you would step forward, and sit in the chairs that were placed in front of the offering table. At the age of twelve I didn't quite understand whether I should be praying to join the church or for "my religion." I didn't know what would be the sign that I had received my religion when I was praying. Later I understood to pray for your "religion" meant to have a salvation experience with the Lord. I wanted both of them but was too afraid to go forward. I sat on the mourner's bench every night hoping for my religion to come. The last day of the revival service, I asked Jesus to come into my heart since the religion I had been praying for never did come. Immediately a river of tears flowed and I began to experience an inner peace. Then the Lord gave me an inner assurance that it was now acceptable to join the church. Many believed that the emotional experience was the sign that they had received their religion (also known as being "born again"). If the older folks thought their child had not received his religion (when he became a member of the church) they would send him back to the mourner's bench to tarry some more. This was another tradition that was passed on from one generation to another.

How many "members" are in church today because of the traditions passed on by their parents? The Bible tells us in Matthew 15:3, "But He answered and said unto them, why do ye also transgress the commandment of God by your tradition"?

After the revival, everyone who had received his or her religion or joined the church would be baptized in water by submersion. On the same Sunday night, communion was served to every Christian. To distinguish non-Christians from Christians, the women were given white headbands and the men were given white armbands to wear when receiving communion. As I began growing in the knowledge of God, I learned that the most important thing is accepting Jesus in my heart and letting Him baptize me with the precious Holy Spirit so that I can live a victorious life. When we except Jesus as our Lord and Savior we become members of the body of Christ. Therefore, we need to become members of a local church that God has chosen for our spiritual growth. We don't have to pray for our "religion" or "tarry" any longer or even get on a "mourner's bench". All we have to do is ask Jesus to come into our hearts and forgive us of our sins. We don't have to tarry no more Jesus has already paid the price for our sins. All we have to do is except the work He has done on the cross.

Plan of Salvation

That if thou (meaning you) shall confess (say) with thy mouth the Lord Jesus and believe in thine heart that God has raised Him from the dead, THOU SHALL BE SAVED" (Rom. 10:9).   If you have never asked Jesus into your heart, repeat this prayer below.

A Prayer of Confession

Father, I confess that I am a sinner and I need a Savior. I ask you to forgive me of my sins and to come into my heart. I confess that you are Lord, and I believe that God has raised Jesus from the dead. You said, if I confess with my mouth the Lord Jesus, and I believe in my heart that God raised Jesus from the dead, that I will be saved. I ask you in Jesus name to fill me with the Holy Spirit that you give to every believer that ask. Thank you for coming into my life, and thank you for your precious gift of the Holy Spirit.

If any man thirst, let him come unto me, and
Drink.

John 7:37

There's got to Be More

During my years of being saved, I felt I had heard nearly every Bible story that had been told because many were preached over and over again. I decided as a child that I would not attend church every Sunday when I became an adult. I thought, "Once saved, always saved." I did not realize that you have to <u>live out</u> that salvation. We are exhorted to, "work out your own salvation with fear and trembling". (Phil. 2:12). When I got saved, I thought I had a ticket in my pocket and I was irreversibly on my way to heaven! I was not taught that I had to develop a relationship with my First Love, Jesus Not having the power of the Holy Ghost in my life after receiving salvation, I began to drift away from God in my early twenties and stopped attending church.

In 1977, I met a young man from Baltimore, Maryland, with whom I fell in love. Ignoring the convictions in my life, I yielded to the temptation of a premarital sexual union. Out of that relationship was born a baby girl. When he asked me to marry him and to move to Maryland where he was stationed in the U.S. Air Force, I said no to him.

There was a fear in my heart of marrying but I could not understand why. The only thing I could say at that moment was that I was not ready. The tears streaming down his face proved how he felt the pain of rejection. This broke his heart and eventually we drifted apart and he move back to Baltimore, Maryland.

Later in my life this drove me to make bad decisions because I did not know how to handle it. Year after year, my life had spiraled downward, and I began to feel that even God didn't love me. I began to settle for the lesser things because I thought this was all that life had to offer. I began to live a rebellious life, especially against God. For three years, I lived in an ungodly relationship with a man I was not married to. I had completely given up on all of my hopes and dreams. In spite of me going my own way God still had a plan for my life more than what I could imagine

Flee Fornication. Every sin that a man doeth is without the body; but he that committed fornication sins against his own body.

I Corinthians 6:18

The Holy Ghost Chase

Even though I physically forsook the church, the Lord did not forsake me. He kept drawing me back to him. I can truthfully say that He leaves the "ninety-nine" and seeks that one that strays. Jesus says, in (Luke 14:4) "What man of you, having a hundred sheep, if he loses one of them, doth not leave the ninety and nine in the wilderness, and go after that which is lost until he finds it"?

The Holy Ghost began whispering in my ear, over and over again, "You need to go back to church." After being convicted, and hearing Him speak repeatedly, I decided that I would go back.

I began to feel like it was something more than just salvation that I needed. I decided to attend a different denomination this time. I had heard about the Holy Ghost, but I thought it was only for what I would call "sanctified people". They were the Christians who attended the Pentecostal churches where women could not wear pants nor cut their hair. I discovered later that the gift of the Holy Ghost was given to anyone who asks for it.

The Lord told His disciples, when He was returning to heaven, that He would send them the gift of the Holy Ghost. He instructed them to wait for the promise: "And, being assembled together with them, commanded them that they should not depart from Jerusalem, but wait for the promise of the Father, which, saith He, ye have heard of me" (Acts 1:4). Before Jesus came, John the Baptist was baptizing people with water once they confessed their sins.

John said: "*I indeed baptize you with water unto repentance: but He that cometh after me is mightier than I, whose shoes I am not worthy to bear: He shall baptize you with the Holy Ghost, and with fire. Whose fan is in His hand, and He will thoroughly purge His floor, and gather His wheat into the garner; but He will burn up the chaff with unquenchable fire*" (Matthew 3:11-12).

Even though the disciples already had Jesus with them, the Lord saw a need for them to have a Comforter when He returned to the Father after His resurrection. He instructed them to wait for the Holy Ghost to come so they could be empowered from on high.

We don't have to wait or tarry like the disciples did because He is here already. All we have to do is ask for, and then receive, that precious gift. We are also His disciples and the promise is for us as well. Jesus said in Acts 2:39, "For the promise is unto you and to your children, and to that are afar off, even as many as the Lord your God shall call".

I tried to live my life by the rules of religion: "You can't do this or that, wear this, or go there." I thought, "If I will do all of that, I will gain brownie points with God". But nothing seemed to change. According to their doctrines, I was not baptized properly because I was not baptized in the "Name of Jesus only". Because I was trying to conform to their doctrine I decided to let them baptize me just in case the Baptist Church might have "missed that rule". Even though I let them baptize me, I was still not quite sure this was the church the Lord wanted me to join. I was willing to do whatever it took to satisfy my spiritual hunger in my soul.

After I had tried to conform to all their rules and doctrines, nothing really changed in my life! I was very determined to find what was missing, so I began seeking God on my own.

After I missed attending this new church a few times, one of the members came to visit me. She asked me, "Why did you stop coming to church"? I said, "I felt that God was leading me in another direction". She said, "I think you left because you wanted to wear your jewelry".

Right at that moment a spirit of condemnation tried to come over me. I felt I had sinned big time because of my lack of understanding of what the Bible said about this. Then, I noticed she wore a ring on her finger, and I asked her why she was wearing jewelry if she believed it was wrong to wear it. She said, "I can't get it off". All of a sudden, God gave me an answer and I said, "My Bible tells me in Mark 9:43, 'And if thine hand offend thee, cut it off: it is better for you to enter into life maimed, than having two hands to go into hell, into the fire that never shall be quenched". Immediately that Word set me free, and the spirit of condemnation left.

You see, the Lord says in John 8:32, "And you shall know the truth, and the truth shall make you free".

That woman was being a Pharisee, trying to put a spirit of condemnation upon me with rules and laws that even she could not live up to. Jesus said, in Matthew 23:4 "For they bind heavy burdens and grievous to be borne, and lay them on men's shoulders; but they themselves will not move them with one of their fingers".

After having that experience, I surrendered to the Lord, and allowed Him to direct me to the church of His choice. I said, "Lord, when I was young, I had to go to the church of my parents' choice, now I'm grown, and I am yours. Where do you want me to go"? A few days later I was invited to an Assemblies of God church. The first Sunday I attended the Assemblies of God church, the pastor was preaching a message on salvation. He said, "There are so many ways people will tell you how to get to heaven, but there is only one way. Jesus is the way, when you ask Jesus in your heart, that's the way to heaven. It's not a bunch of rules and regulations, you can't do this or that, or you can't go here or there. The Holy Spirit will tell you what you can't do or where you can't go". I said, "I need to go and talk to the preacher after the service is over". I said even thou I am a Christian it still seems as if something is missing in my life"! He gently replied, "Do you have any sin in your life that you know of?" I knew I was living with someone to whom I was not married, and that arrangement was a sin.

When I acknowledged the truth, he said unto me, "God wants to use you, but He can't use you like that, and I want you to go to heaven he said". For the very first time, I felt the Love of God like never before. I said, "What must I do?" He said, "Either marry the guy, or get out of it! But I think God has something better for you.

In spite of the home and lifestyle situation I had created, I kept going to church. The more I went and heard the Word of God, the more I desired to live a godly life. It also made me more determine to seek God's will for my life.

The Living Waters

One evening, as I was doing my private devotions, I felt impressed to call my pastor and ask him to pray for me. His wife answered the phone. I told her that I needed prayer and I wanted to see if the pastor could pray for me. She said that he was over at the church working. After I finished talking with her, I drove to the church because I felt an urgency to go right then! I sensed that when he would pray for me something was going to happen. When I got to the church, he and several men were moving some things around in his office. It was around 8:30 p.m. when I arrived. I was a little hesitant about going so late but there was a sense of urgency that compel me to go right then. When he answered the door the look on his face signaled, "This has to be very important." The Holy Spirit always does things in decency and in proper order. Though, let us not forget, God sees our hearts and our intentions! The Lord had set the whole thing up because there were others working with him that night and therefore we were not alone.

I said, "Rev. Allen, as I was praying tonight, the Lord impressed upon my heart to call you and ask you to pray for me. I called your home and your wife said that you and some other members were over at the church working. After I finished talking with her, I still felt this urgency in my spirit that I needed you to pray for me right now." I said, "There's something else I need from the Lord but I don't know what it is." He looked at his watch, and his facial expression seemed to say, "Right <u>now</u>?" Then he invited me in and said to me, "Loretta, you need the baptism of the Holy Spirit!" I said, "How do you get it?" He said, "All you have to do is ask God to fill you and then begin to praise Him". I said, "Can the Lord fill me sitting down"? He said, "You can receive it anywhere: sitting down, kneeling, or even driving your car".

Then Rev. Allen asked one of the workers to come over and agree with him in prayer that God would fill me with the Holy Ghost (Spirit). After they prayed, he told me to lift up my hands and to begin praising the Lord. Earlier that day, I had asked the Lord Himself to fill me, so I would know it was He who was granting my request. As I began to lift up my hands and praise the Lord, all of a sudden, my stomach began to burn with the fire of God and up from my belly flowed "living waters as the scripture said. I began to speak in tongues; a heavenly language. As I was praying in tongues, Rev. Allen returned and encouraged me by saying excitedly, "Loretta, get way down in that water!"! The Lord gloriously filled me that night with the Holy Ghost and with fire.

When I returned home that night, the devil tried to tell me that I was not filled with the Holy Ghost. When I open my bible to read the first scripture my eyes fell on was Matthew 3:11 which says, "*I indeed baptize you with water unto repentance: but he that cometh after me is mightier than I, whose shoes I am not worthy to bear: he shall baptize you with the Holy Ghost, and with fire*". After I read that scripture a peace came over me and it settled any doubt or arguments that the baptism had not actually happened. Then I understood what I had just experienced. This is what I had been searching for all those years and I had finally found it! This was the power I was missing in my life after I had received my salvation! After I had been saved, I knew there was something more. I believe that if I had received the Holy Ghost immediately after I was saved, I would have that power to live a more victorious life. There are many people who once invited Jesus into their hearts and, because they didn't receive the Power of the baptism of the Holy Ghost, has drifted back into the world and are enslaved by and in bondage to all types of sins.

But ye shall receive power, after that the Holy Ghost
is come upon you: and ye shall be witnesses unto me
both in Jerusalem, and in all Judea, and in Samaria,
and unto the uttermost part of the earth.

Acts 1:8

The Fire Burns Up the Chaff

After the Lord filled me with the Holy Spirit, He began to purge me from ungodly soul ties. I could no longer live in sin and feel comfortable! The Holy Spirit kept convicting me, day after day, to help bring me out of that lifestyle. He was the one making me feel badly about "living in sin. "The Lord said in John 16:7–8, "*Nevertheless I tell you the truth. It is to your advantage that I go away; for if I do not go away the Helper will not come to you; but if I depart, I will send Him to you, and when He has come He will convict the world of sin, and of righteousness, and of judgment*". The longer I chose to stay in that situation, the harder things seemed to get. It seemed the more I prayed, the more the heavens "became brass". My prayers felt like they were getting no farther than the ceiling. The Lord permitted the conviction so that I would repent and turn from my sin and follow in His steps. Instead of yielding to the convicting power of the Holy Spirit, I started running from God. I left my home for a few days, trying to get away from the things that seemed to haunt me. I decided to stay with a friend of mine for a few days (Like Jonah running to Tarshish).

The first night I was at my girlfriend's house guess who showed up? Yes, the presence of the Lord in a tangible way. As I was trying to go to sleep I kept tossing and turning throughout the night. The Lord would not let me sleep! Since I could not go to sleep I got up, sat on the side of the bed, and began talking to the Lord. I said, "Lord, why don't you hear my prayers, why don't you just save me out of this situation"? It seemed like the heavens had become brass and my prayers was getting no further than the ceiling. As I was talking to the Lord, I opened my Bible, and it fell open to Isaiah 59:1–2 which says, "*My hand is not too shortened that it cannot save, nor my ear is too heavy where I cannot hear you, but your sins have hid your God's face where He cannot hear*". The handwriting was truly on the wall! I just sat there in awe of how the Lord spoke to me so directly out of His Word! Then the Lord said, "I want you out of the situation, but not out of your home".

Even though I went back home the next day I was still afraid of letting go of the relationship because I didn't have a job to support four kids and myself. While I was thinking on this, the Lord told me to turn to Matthew 7:7, which says, "*Ask and it shall be given, seek and ye shall find, knock and the door shall be opened*".

Immediately I fell on my knees and asked the Lord to give me a job! The next day I received employment as a secretary at a preschool center!

After hearing the Lord speak so clearly to me, you would think I would give immediate obedience to the Lord in my life. But, after I started working on my job, the conviction was not as strong as it was before. I thought, "Maybe things are starting to go in my favor now"! So, I suppressed the "bad situation" and put it in the back of my mind. God had given me a blessing, and with ingratitude I did not completely surrender to my Maker and Father.

One day, out of the blue, I begin to feel the presence of the Holy Spirit entered my office. I began to feel a miserable feeling, and the peace of God began to leave me. I was unable to shake this feeling off; so, I left work for the rest of the day. As I was on my way home, I decided to go and talk to the pastor again. Instead the youth pastor counseled me because the senior pastor was gone. Since he had no knowledge of my situation I thought he would tell me something totally different that would make me feel better. I said, "I know that I have the Lord in my life, but I have no peace"! He said, "Do you have any sin in your life that you know of"? We were back to the same question that the senior pastor asked me when I first talked to him! I forgot that he had the same Holy Spirit the pastor had. It was the Holy Spirit talking directly through him to me.

I said, "I'm not committing fornication anymore with the man I live with. "Then he said, "Well, are you still 'living in sin"? "The Lord says, in I Thessalonians 5:22, "*Abstain from the appearance of evil.*" He said, "What does it look like to the public? They don't know that you are not sleeping with him"! He said, "When you get out of it, then you will begin to feel God's peace. "I was really under conviction after the truth had been revealed to me. I was so miserable living in those circumstances, and I knew that night I had to make a life-changing decision or something worse was going to happen to me. That night, I told the man with whom I was living with that we had to get married because I could no longer "live in sin". He promised me that we were going to marry but not right away!

While I was waiting, hoping and praying for him to be ready for marriage, something strange began happening to me! One night I was awakened by the sound of a loud trumpet blast! I sat up in the bed, and a still small voice said, "Was that the trumpet? And was that the rapture"? Immediately, the Scripture came back to me in I Thessalonians 4:16–17 that says, "*For the Lord Himself will descend from heaven with a shout with the voice of an archangel and with the trumpet of God! And the dead in Christ shall rise first, then we, who are alive and remain, shall be caught up together with them in the clouds to meet the Lord in the air and thus shall we always be with the Lord*"! I thought, "Oh no! I've missed the rapture!" Fear began to grip me and my sin began condemning me, "Yes, you have been left behind"! There was no way I could convince myself that I was ready, and I should not have been left behind! I was reminded of how the Lord had been dealing with me over and over again through His love kindness. He had been speaking through His Word to me, saying, *"Flee fornication, every sin that a man does is outside the body, but he who commits fornication sins against his own body,* I Corinthians 6:18 ".

I had resisted the chastening of the Lord time after time. I was afraid to look into my kids' room to see if they had been rapture. I knew if the rapture had taken place, they would have been taken up! I began to pray, "Oh Lord, please give me another chance and I'll obey you!" All of a sudden, I began to hear my baby cry! I jumped up and ran in the kids' room, and thanked God they were still there!

It was then that I began to realize how the Lord was warning me to be ready at all times because the rapture could take place any time! I did not want my present situation to cause me to be left behind! When we become "born again" we should not practice or live an unholy lifestyle. The Lord warns us not to be deceived. He knew that some people would think that they could live sinful lifestyles and still consider themselves "Christians". We are considered unrighteous in God's sight when we live this non-Christ like lifestyle. When we become born again, the Lord washes us from all of our sin and there is no way we can, or should be, living that way. I Corinthians 6:11 says, "Such were some of you, but you were washed, but you were sanctified, but you were justified in the name of the Lord Jesus and by the Spirit of our God." Remember, the Lord said, "Watch therefore, for you do not know what hour your Lord is coming" (Matthew 24:42).

I was so happy that the rapture had not taken place and the Lord was giving me another chance to obey him. After having that experience, I was left with a sobering feeling that "God is not playing". The next night I began separating myself by sleeping in another room "until we got married".

After I started making steps to obey the Lord, the Holy Spirit said, "Why don't you ask God if this man is to be your husband"? He said, "Just because you are living with him, doesn't mean that he is your husband"!

Then the Lord reminded me of the story of the woman at the well. He said unto her, "Go, call thy husband, and come hither". The woman answered and said, 'I have no husband". Jesus said unto her, "Thou hast well said, I have no husband. For thou hast had five husbands and he whom thou now hast is not thy husband, in that saidst thou truly".

We humans always desperately want to choose our mate ourselves, but when we leave it up to God, He chooses our best mate. The same night the Lord showed me in a dream that this man, whom I was living with, was not my husband! When I woke up I noticed my Bible was lying open at the foot of my bed. I picked it up and it was already opened to II Corinthians 6:14 which say "*Do not be unequally yoked with unbelievers*".

The Lord always warns us before we do something that is not His will! He also leaves the choice to obey Him up to us because we have a will! But He is always there to help us make the right choice. When we are willing and obedient, then we can receive the blessing.

After all of this time of me waiting he finally ask me to married him but I chose to obey God's Word and to walk with Him. I said to him, "My Lord does not want me to be unequally yoked." He said, "Well, you can live your way and I'll live my way"!

Do you see how Satan was tempting me? Then I realized that God had given me His strength, boldness, and confidence to release myself from this relationship! I said, "That's exactly what the Lord is talking about when He says unequally yoked".

From that moment on I decided that I was no longer going to live in sin, but I was going to live my life for the Lord. That very night I repented of the lifestyle I had been living while being a Christian. Then I asked God to provide a place for him to live. The next day he found a place and moved out! There was no animosity between us because this was the Lord's doing! Immediately I felt a release in my spirit and that everything was going to be all right!

When the Lord tells you to do something He gives you the grace to do it. That's why you need to obey while the grace is there because when the grace lifts you cannot do it in your own ability.

When I got home that afternoon, I felt God's presence in a very special way! My home had such a peaceful atmosphere. I said, "Well, Lord, now it's only you, my children, and I who are in this home!" That night I began to experience the peace that my pastor told me I would receive as soon as I came out of my willful sin! It felt like a bucket of honey being poured over my head, and it flowed down to the tips of my toes! It was this peace that the Lord talks about that passes all understanding. "*And the peace of God that passes all understanding shall keep your hearts and minds through Christ Jesus*" (Philippians 4:7). It literally made me "drunk" in the spirit. It was like a supernatural high that kept a smile on my face all the time.

When I went to work the next day one of my co-workers said to me "whatever that is you are on give me some of that because you are always smiling". I said, "It's that new wine that Jesus gives".

He Brought Me Out to Bring Me In

It was not easy being a single parent after the Lord brought me out. When anyone is used to having someone else, who is not there anymore, they have to learn to depend on God and Him alone. When the Lord brings us out, He wants us to cut all ties. Only the Lord can cut the spiritual dependency ties and He will give us the ability to cut the natural ties. If we don't cut all ties, and there is any dependency left in the relationship, we can be seduced back into bondage.

The day I was tempted to reach back into that relationship, the Lord spoke to me through his word in Galatians 5:1 which says, "*Stand fast therefore in the liberty wherewith Christ has made you free and be not entangled again with the yoke of bondage.*" Then He gave me a closure to the relationship when I mYbegin to read Luke 9:62 which states "*No one, having put his hand to the plow, and looking back, is fit for the kingdom of God.*" Then I knew it was over and it was time to completely move on.

Now the Lord finally had me completely to Himself. He was now ready to reveal Himself to me. I knew of Him but didn't know Him personally. So, He led me to a church where I could begin to grow spiritually and learn more about Him. He brought me out to bring me in. He gave me pastors that did not compromise the Word of God, but spoke the truth. As I began to pray and study the Bible, the Lord began to reveal His truths to me.

It is very important to let God lead us to the church of His choice! He knows exactly what we need at this time of our spiritual lives. The church the Lord leads you to will be equipped to meet your spiritual needs. If the house of worship we are now attending is not challenging our spiritual growth, we need to begin seeking God in this area to see where the Lord is telling us to go. I don't feel God cares so much about where we're worshiping, but He does care about how we are getting feed and are we growing! If your spiritual growth is still where it was ten years ago, you need to ask for new pastures in which to be "shepherded."

My Sheep hear my voice, and I know them and they
follow me.

John 10:27

Fear thou not; for I am with thee: Be not dismayed; for I am thy God: I will strengthen thee; yea, I will help thee; Yea, I will uphold thee with the right hand of my righteousness.

Isaiah 41:10

God Reveals His Protection

The first thing He revealed to me about Himself was that He was well able to take care of me all by Himself. He proved this to me one night when an unusual thing happened.

After I had put the kids to bed, and had been asleep for a while, the Lord woke me up and began spiritually tugging on me. As I sat up, He said, in a still small voice, "Listen." I was still sleepy so I laid back down. Then he pulled me up again, and said a second time, "Listen." As I sat up in the bed, I heard a noise coming from inside the front of the house.

As I attempted to get up, I noticed there was a belt lying at the foot of my bed. When I grabbed the belt, I seemed to be led by a strong force down the hallway. I heard the noise coming from my bathroom, and when I looked, I saw someone trying to get through the window! I took the belt and struck the paneling on the wall. As soon as the intruder heard the noise, he took off running! The Lord said, "Didn't that belt made a sound like a gun?" He said, "I use the simplest things for weapons." I was shaking from the power of God that was upon me. I said, "Lord, you are something else! You made that belt sound just like a gun! That person thought I shot at them!" Then I said, "Lord what do I do now?" He said, "Read Psalm 91." As I began to read each word, my whole body began to shake under the power of God!

It states, "*He that dwelleth in the secret place of the most high shall abide under the shadow of the almighty. I will say of the Lord He is my refuge and my fortress, my God in Him will I trust. Surely He shall deliver me from the snare of the fowler and from the noiselence pestilence. He will cover me with his feathers under His wings will I trust. His truth shall be my shield and buckler. I will not fear for the terror by night, nor for the arrow that flieth by day nor for the pestilence that walketh in darkness for the destruction that wastes at noonday. A thousand shall fall at thy side; ten thousand at thy right hand but it shall not come nigh thee. Only with my eyes will I behold and see the reward of the wicked because thou hast made the Lord thy refuge even the most High thy habitation. There shall no evil befall thee neither shall any plague come nigh thy dwelling. For He shall give his angels charge over thee to keep thee in all thou ways. They shall bear thee up in their hands lest thou dash thy foot against a stone. Thou shalt tread upon the lion and adder. The young lion and dragon shalt thou trample under feet. Because He hath set his love upon me therefore will I deliver him: I will set him upon high because he has known my name.*

He shall call upon me and I will answer him: I will be with him in trouble: I will deliver him and honor him. With long life will I satisfy him and show him my salvation."

Immediately after I finished reading the chapter, a supernatural peace came over me and the shaking stopped. Right at that moment, I knew that I had been in the presence of the Lord.

The Healing Power of God

The Lord revealed to me His power to heal. I had read of many stories in the bible of miracles of healing but I did know Him as my Healer.

One day I became very ill from an infection that had formed in my body. As the inflammation began spreading throughout my body, I began losing weight and became very weak. It dramatically affected my gums, causing them to become discolored. When I could eat, the food would taste bitter. Then a few minutes later I would feel like I hadn't eaten anything. As I was lying in bed one night, I asked the Lord to show me what was wrong, and what was happening to me. When I fell to sleep the Lord showed me in a dream a very large snake that was chasing me. Then he handed me a very large knife to cut off its head. After I cut its head off I looked down inside the snake's body, and I saw all of the food I had been eating! I woke up and began to ponder the dream. I said, "Lord, what does that mean"? He said, "You have poison in your body and the poison is eating up your food."

The next night my face begins to swell and my gums began to bleed excessively. I was weak, scared and did not know what to do. I did not have a phone to call anyone to help me so I woke my son up to go to the neighbor's house to ask her to take me to the hospital. It was very cold and rainy that night but I had to see a doctor because of the bleeding. What was so ironic when we got to the hospital, we could not even get in because the emergency doors were locked though they were normally open twenty-four hours. I felt like the devil was trying to kill me but I knew the Lord was with me and he had a plan for my life!

Since we could not get in, we went back home and called my mother to ask her to come over. My mother (and my step-grandmother, Irma Payne) came over to help me. They prayed for me, and put an ice pack on my face to take the swelling down. Then they gave me some medicine to help get the bleeding under control.

The next day one of my girlfriends came over. (She is a very special person who loves the Lord with all of her heart). Barbara and I grew up together and were classmates. When we both became Christians, we were in similar situations. We would pray together, go to church together, and encourage one another when we needed it. She was always sensitive to the Lord, and proved to be obedient when she came the next day to take us to church. When she saw that I was not feeling very well, she asked to take my kids to church so that I could rest. After she left, my neighbor that had taken me to the hospital came to check on how I was doing. She noticed I was a little better but still looked weak so she suggested that I let her call someone from my church to come and pray for me. The Lord brought to my mind a lady from our church that had the gift of healing operating in her prayer life. While my neighbor went to her house to Madeline, the Lord told me to, "Get up, and straighten up the room!" I said, "Lord, I can't! I'm too weak'! He said, "If you get up, I'll strengthen you"! I continued lying there, waiting for the lady to come. The Lord said, "She is not coming until you get up!" Then I began to think about how the Lord always asks us to do something to activate our miracle. As I began to rise from my bed, the Lord began to strengthen me! As soon as I finished cleaning, and was about to get back into bed, the doorbell rang! When the lady came in, she realized that I was very sick and needed a special touch from the Lord! She said she had never seen anything like she was witnessing that day. She said, "Let's kneel down here and ask God what is wrong with you." She prayed for a few minutes and then she paused in silence. Then she said to me, "I feel in my spirit that you need to do something no later than tomorrow!" Then anxiety and fear swept over me and I groaned, "What am I going to do"? Then she said, "I don't know, but the Lord knows what to do"! She said, "He has given us the knowledge to know that there is something desperately wrong, so let's kneel back down and ask Him for wisdom to know what to do". As she began to pray, she thanked God for His knowledge, and then she asked Him for wisdom. Suddenly, I began to feel the healing virtue from God flowing into my arm. I was instantly healed? I opened my eyes and looked at her as this was happening to me. With her eyes closed, and a smile on her face, she began to thank God for His presence and for healing me! After the Spirit of God ceased flowing and we finished praying, I jumped to my feet and said with amazement,

"I am healed"! She then said, with confidence, "I know you are"! I was supernaturally healed by the power of God. God revealed to me that day that He is the true healer.

After she left I went to look in the mirror, and to my surprise, the color of my gums had gone back to its natural hue. I said, in a soft whisper full of amazement, "I am healed". Then the Lord spoke in a still, small voice, "Nothing but the blood of Jesus washes away sin and diseases." I began to joyfully shout and praise God! He had made the promise mine! Shortly after the Lord performed this miracle, she left and my girlfriend came back with the kids. I thought to myself, "The Lord always does things in order!" He had Barbara come and take my kids to church, and get them out of the way, so He could perform a miracle in my life. She looked at me and said, "What happened you have a glow all over you"? I said to her, "I'm healed"! She answered, "I know that you are because you sure look like it! Praise the Lord"! Praise the Lord, indeed!

Give Me My Own King

After I had been serving the Lord for about a year and a half, I started allowing a spirit of discontent to come into my life. The Lord had begun revealing Himself to me in awesome ways, but I began getting frustrated with having to carry all of the responsibilities of a single parent. I began to take my eyes off God, and I started wanting someone to physically be there to help share my responsibilities. I started asking the Lord to send me a husband. I felt that that would solve my problems. It became my prayer, over and over, every day and night.

One Sunday evening I was unable to attend our church service. I was very disappointed because I looked forward to being in the worship service on Sunday. So, that afternoon, I decided that I would just have a good talk with the Lord and tell Him what was on my heart.

As I went outside to take in the clothes off of the clothesline I began to converse with the Lord. I said, "Lord, I'm tired of being a single parent, and having all the responsibilities of washing, cooking, cleaning, and taking care of the kids"! The Lord said, "If you hold on, I'm going to send you someone to help you with all of that"! Immediately I thought the Lord was going to send me a husband. I did not know that I was not ready for a husband because the Lord wanted to do some more things in my life!

When I got into the house and went to put the clothes away, the Lord said, "Turn your television on". I said, "Why should I turn the television on? I don't have cable"! I said, "If I had cable, I would be watching our church tonight"! When I came back through the den the Lord said again, "Turn your television on"! I the television on, and the picture was very snowy where there was no image showing. All of a sudden, the picture began to clear up right before my eyes! There was my Pastor saying these words, "There is someone watching by way of television and you are praying for a companion"! He said, "And you are doing all the washing, cooking, and cleaning, but if you hold on God is going to send someone to help you with all of that"! After he said those words, the picture began to slowly fade out, and turn snowy again with no picture showing at all! I was so amazed at the miracle that the Lord performed just to send a word of confirmation to me! As I stood there in amazement, the power of God came over me and I began to praise Him! I was so excited that God had heard my prayer, and I was now going to receive the desire of my heart.

Set Up to Set Back

Shortly after receiving my word from the Lord, the devil sought out to "set me up" again. Satan sent back into my life someone whom I had dated when I was not a Christian.

During our conversation, I shared with him how God had changed my life. He seemed to be excited and interested while hearing about my new Christian experience. After having been in and out of wrong relationships, I had become vulnerable. I had not given God time to heal me emotionally from past relationships. That was the reason I still felt the need to have someone in my life. I thought it would fill that void that never seemed to relent. Sometimes healing comes instantaneously but sometimes it is a process. It really depends on the individual and how the Lord desires to heal. If you are not totally healed from past relationships, you can carry all that baggage into the next relationship. If you are not fully healed, you can make wrong choices because of wrong motives.

One day, the devil put it in this man's heart to ask me if he could come and visit me. Without praying about it or realizing that it was a set up, I told him he could.

When I got home from work, I got an impression that I needed to pray. As I did, I began to repent for not inquiring of the Lord concerning this decision that I had made. After I turned my will over to the Lord, I felt a great peace come over me. I waited from 7:00 p.m. until 10:00 p.m., and he never showed up or called. I was a little disappointed but I was thankful that God's will was done! It was so powerful that the children of Israel asked Moses to speak to them on their behalf in answer to God's resounding reverberations! They would say "Moses, you speak with us, and we will hear; but let not God speak with us lest we die! In Exodus 20:18–19 it says, "*Now all the people witnessed the thundering, the lightning flashes, the sound of the trumpet and the mountain smoking and when the people saw it, they trembled and stood afar off.*

The next day, I received a phone call from Satan's counterfeit "soul mate" and all of my excitement of talking with him was completely gone! He said, "I tried to come to your house last night, but as I got closer a fear came over me, and something would not let me come!" I said, "That was truly God because I asked Him if it was not His will for you to come, do not let you come. He said, "I heard that you go to that Assembly of God church where that preacher is preaching against fornication." I said, "Yes, I do, and the Bible speaks against it too!" It says in I Corinthians 6:18, "*Flee Fornication; every sin that a man doeth is without the body; but he that committed fornication sinneth against his own body. What? Know ye not that your body is the temple of the Holy Ghost which is in you, which ye have of God, and ye are not your own.*" I told him that the Lord did not want me to pursue this relationship any further. Then he said, "I hope you find the person you are looking for".

A few months later, the Lord confirmed to me that I had made the right choice by obeying Him in not pursuing that relationship! He sent a lady to me who had started dating this same man a few months later.

She said to me, "Loretta, you better be glad that you did not get tangled up in a relationship with this guy! She said, "I let him move into my house and he became violent with me until I had to let him go!" Immediately, the Lord reminded me of the dream that He had given me. The Lord showed me this man's heart and what he was really like. Then I knew God had protected me again from a situation that might have destroyed my life. I thank the Lord for His intervention! God can warn us in our dreams just as Joseph, Jesus' earthly father, was told to flee from Herod to protect the Christ child.

After I had received the word that God was going to send someone to help me, I still was anticipating that it was going to be soon. We can allow anxiety and frustration to get in the way of God's plan. The Lord said in Philippians 4:6– 7, "*Be anxious for nothing, but in everything by prayer and supplication with thanksgiving, let your requests be made known to God; and the peace of God, which surpasses all understanding, will guard your hearts and minds through Christ Jesus*".

The devil didn't just stop trying to deter God's plan at that point. He sent another man into my life. He seemed to fit that description of what I had prayed for. Not only what I had prayed for but also it looked like the word I had received. He was very willing to help me with all the responsibilities I had as a single parent. This was too good to be true and it seemed to be a God-inspired solution. The responsibilities that I had been carrying began to diminish. I was so mesmerized by the things that this man contributed to my family, that I lost focus on what the Lord was trying to do in my life. I thought this was the answer to my prayers. I began to settle for it because I felt that it couldn't get any better than this. Of course, he was not a believer, so I had doubts, but I was encouraged by some of my Christian friends who were saying to me, "I wouldn't let that good man get away"! They saw all the things he was doing for me and thought it was wonderful. They saw how beautiful my yard looked, how clean my car stayed, and how he would attend church with me every Sunday! I didn't realize that I was falling in love with the things he was doing but not with him. Ask yourself that question, "Did I fall in love with this person or in love with the things he or she possesses that would benefit me"!

The Lord tried to intercept this by sending a precious lady into my life from Dallas, Texas. He sent her and her family to Louisiana for "a special assignment". The moment I met Rachel I felt a kindred spirit. She felt a special burden in her heart to help my family and me. She would come over once a week to help cook, clean, and give me a break for some "me" time. I did not realize that this was the promise that God was fulfilling when He said, through my pastor, that He was going to send SOMEONE to help me. I took this word and went with it and presumed that God was talking about a husband. Since I assumed that God was talking about a husband the devil blinded me by using the things this man was doing for me to draw me away from the will of God. God's ways are not our ways. He said in Isaiah 55:8, "*For my thoughts are not your thoughts, nor are your ways my ways. For as the heavens are higher than the earth, so are my ways higher than your ways, and my thoughts than your thoughts*".

I did not give the Lord the chance to reveal himself as my provider. I thought having a husband was the only way God could provide for me and my family. I was overlooking the true gift the Lord had given to us.

Before I got deeper into the relationship with this man the Lord sent someone to tell me that he was not the one for me! I didn't accept it because I felt she was jealous and was trying to keep me from what I thought was a blessing.

I married him despite the warning the Lord was giving me. I met him in March and Married him in May and knew nothing about him.

A few weeks into my marriage, I found out that my husband had an addiction to alcohol. I was devastated and did not know what to do!" I had been blind to the signs that were given to me because of my fleshly desires and frantic manipulations. I had taken my eyes off the Lord as my provider. The Lord says in James 1:14, "*But each one is tempted when he is drawn away by his own desires and enticed.*" I felt like I went from the frying pan into the fire. I said, "Lord, what happened? I thought you sent this man to me"! He spoke these words to me, "YOU MARRIED UNEQUALLY YOKED!!" Those very words pierce my soul! At that moment, I felt trapped, and even betrayed, and thought I had no way out. The Lord began to remind me of the children of Israel, when they were crying out for a king and no longer wanted God to lead them. He said to me, "I had brought you out time after time from wrong relationships because I wanted to prove to you that I was everything you needed"! He said, "I wanted to be your king, but you wanted another"! I knew I had broken my "First Love's" heart. I began to weep bitter and sorrowful tears because I had rejected the Lord. At that moment, I repented to the Lord for my rebellion and then I asked Him to bring deliverance!

That same night the Lord gave me a vision. I saw myself sitting in His hand and His hand was moving slowly through a storm. At the very end of the storm, He let down the most beautiful rainbow right in front of me. While I was admiring all the beautiful colors He let me see behind it. I saw behind the rainbow a long table with two angels on standing on each side of the table. On the table there were two birthday cakes and other party stuff. I said to myself, "They are giving someone a party". As I continue checking out this scene I saw my husband sitting at the end of the table. When I awoke from the vision the Lord said to me, "Get up, and write the vision down!" As I began to write, I said, "Lord, what does that rainbow represent"? He said, "Covenant promise, this night I promise I'm going to bring you deliverance". I said, "What do the two cakes represent"? He said, "A natural birth and a spiritual birth". Lastly, I ask, "Why was my husband sitting at the end of the table"? The

Lord said, "I am going to save him at the end of his life'.

The next day when I went to church before Pastor Allen begin preaching he held up it bible and said, "The Holy Ghost gave me a message to preach "<u>Great Deliverance Giveth to His Anointed</u>". He said, The Lord may have dropped a promise in your heart during the night, but that is not saying that you won't have to go through the storm but hold on to the promise it will bring you to the other side. He said don't jump ship!

When the Lord gave me this promise, that He was going to deliver me, He did not tell me how He was going to do it. Neither did He tell me what I was going to have to go through before I would receive the promise. My anchor during the storm was the very words He had spoken to my heart: "I will bring deliverance"! I held onto that promise, and that promise is truly speaking today!

God is not a man that He should lie, nor the son of man that He should repent, if HE said it, HE will do it; if HE spoke it, HE will bring it to pass."

Numbers 23:19

His Love Sustained Me

One Sunday morning, during church, I decided that I would sit on the front row. Later on, during the service, my husband came in and stood right beside me. He put his arms around my waist and passionately began to hug me. It felt that every bit of his weight was hanging on me. I was so embarrassed and I sensed that everyone in church was watching. Me, and they were! They knew that he was struggling with alcoholism. I said, "Lord, what am I to do"? Surprisingly the Lord said to me, "Hug him back". As I can recall, the Lord never allowed his behavior to get out of hand where it brought attention that would cause the service to be disrupted at any time. I had to trust the Lord to take care of every situation that arose because I never knew what action he would take under the influence of alcohol. After I put my arms around him, the Lord said to me, "Loretta, there are a lot of people in this church who are in the same condition as your husband". He said, "Sin is sin to me, there is no big or little sin or black or white. There are liars, fornicators, and adulterers sitting right in your midst that you don't know anything about. If you have un-forgiveness toward him, neither you nor they are any better than he". As the Lord was talking to me, I stood there with my arms around him and wept. This humbled me in a way that even I could not believe myself! The Lord said to me "You are going to teach the body of Christ how to love unconditionally. If you shun him, they will shun him; if you pull close to him, they will reach out to him". I said, "Lord, I can't do that". He said, "I know you can't. Let Me do it through you!" I said, "Okay, Lord, do it". From then on, no matter what condition my husband was in, when he came to church, the Lord gave me the strength and ability to demonstrate God's love. God used this trial to change my life in awesome ways. It drove me closer to God than ever before. I had to spend much time in prayer and in the Word, to deal with the battle I was facing. The Lord had promised me deliverance and I was determined to hold on to the promise until it was fulfilled.

There were times I just wanted to get out of the marriage but I did not have the ability to leave. I could not understand why I could not just walk out like others had done in their marriages. Even through the hardest trials, I did not have it in me to leave.

Later on, the Lord reminded me of the promise He gave me that He was going to deliver me. He said, "The night I gave you that promise, I made a covenant with you, and now you and I are in covenant". He said, "A covenant is an agreement between two people". I asked, "What is my part of the agreement"? He said, "Your part is to go through the storm, and my part is to bring the deliverance". I was now in covenant with God, that's why I did not have the ability to leave the marriage. When I repented of marrying into an "unequally yoked" situation that night, the Lord made a covenant with me to bring me out.

As the years slowly went by, the promise seemed to be a long time in coming. There were times I grew weary and started questioning the Lord by saying, "How long, oh Lord, how long"? One morning He answered me through a song that came forth from

lips, "In His time He makes all things beautiful!

I am the light of this world: he that followeth me shall not walk in darkness, but shall have the light of life.

John 8:12

For the Lord see not as man seethed; for man looks on the outward appearance, but the Lord looketh on the heart.

I Samuel 16:7

Deal with the Real Issue

During our thirteen years of being married, my husband always seemed insecure about our relationship. I noticed, once a year, he would ask me if I had someone else in my life. I could not understand what made him feel that way because I was always faithful to him. I tried assuring him that I had no one else except the Lord, but he continued feeling that way. The only thing I felt that could make him feel insecure was his continuing addiction.

The last time I was confronted with him asking me this question, I began to realize that maybe I should take this more serious and talk to the Lord about it. This particular night I got up and went in my prayer room to have a talk with the Lord. I said, "Lord why does he always ask me that"? To my surprise, the Lord said to me, "It's in your heart".

I was completely shocked. I said, "Who's in my heart"? Then the Lord became silent and said no more. I could not imagine, or begin to think, that after all these years of marriage I could have someone else in my heart! How could this happen to a person who was very faithful to God and her husband for these thirteen years? I thought, "After all these years, surely I love my husband"!

If the Lord says that something is in your heart, it's in your heart.

The next day, to my surprise, I received an unexpected call from Baltimore, Maryland, from my daughter's father whom I had not seen, or heard from, in eighteen years! When I heard his voice something came alive in my heart that brought tears to my eyes! My head could not understand what was happening in my heart! I literally wanted to say, "I still love you"! but my head was saying, "No, you can't say that, You're married"! I just got choked up and was silent for a minute or two. When I did speak I told him I had to go and I hung up the phone. I was afraid of what I was feeling at the moment. Just hearing his voice, I felt a love that I had not felt in a long time. I thought to myself, "Where is this coming from and why now"? The scary part was I begin to realize I had not ever felt those type of feelings for the man I was married to.

After I hung the phone up. As I sat silently at my desk pondering on what had just happen the Lord spoke to me in a still small voice. He said, "That's the person who is in your heart, and you have never had put closure to that relationship, you never had let him go in your heart. All of the other relationships that God brought me out of had not affected me like this. I began to ask the Lord, "What is the difference"? The Lord said, "The difference is that he was the person with whom you were in love. The other relationships were based off of wrong motives". I said, "Oh no! What am I going to do? I am married, but in love with another man"! I could not understand why after all these years; I did not know this!

The Lord said to me, "You did not know this because it was suppressed by your subsequent relationships. He said, I uncovered it so you would know the issue that had been lying dormant but buried alive. I could not understand, after so many years, why the Lord was now allowing this to come up in my life!

I remembered when I began to repent for marrying unequally yoked; the Lord had given me a word through my pastor, "GREAT DELIVERANCE GIVETH HE TO HIS ANNOINTED ONE". It was not only bringing me out of my situation but was trying to bring deliverance in my soul.

When the Lord made a covenant with me that He was going to bring me deliverance, He also said He was not going to take me out but He was going to process me. The process had now started and it started with the Lord dealing with my heart.

There are so many Marry people that are in relationships that are not one with their mates because they need to be delivered in their soul. The next few days, I spent time seeking the Lord about what to do with this, and how to let go. I began to feel guilty and ashamed that the person I was married to was not the person I was truly in love with. I had to repent of living a lie all those years, of living in deception. After I repented of the untruth that I had been living as a Christian and as a wife, the Lord started the process of deliverance in my life. I felt that this was the time to allow God to deal with these issues so that He could minister healing and deliverance to my marriage.

The next step the Lord gave me was to deal honestly with Him. As I began to seek the Lord for guidance, He dropped into my heart Psalms 28:13 "*He who covers his sins will not prosper, but whoever confesses and forsakes them, will have mercy*".

After having this experience, I was ready to deal with it, no matter what it took. In a situation like this, we must have the wisdom of God and His timing.

In Proverbs 3:6 it says "*In all your ways acknowledge Him and He will direct your path*". Little did I know the Lord would be opening the door sooner than I thought!

A few days later, my husband woke up one night and asked me again, did I have someone else? As I was lying down thinking about all of this, the Lord said, "It's time to deal with the real issue. At that moment I felt that this was going to be the day for our breakthrough. My husband got up, and went to the kitchen to make coffee. A few minutes later I got up, and went into the kitchen where he was. I opened my Bible and laid it on the table.

As I sat at the table waiting for a cup of coffee, I said, "Lord, is it really time for me to talk to him about this"? As I began to look down at the Bible that was open in front of me, a Scripture in Psalms seemed to jump out at me: "*You have heard the desire of the humble and you will prepare his heart. You will cause your ear to hear*" (Psalms 10:17).

Then the Lord said to me, "You can tell him". The Lord allowed me to open up and share my heart with my husband.

After I had finished talking, he said, "I want to ask you just one question, do you still love your daughter's daddy"? I really didn't think I should answer that because I didn't know how he was going to say if I really tell him the truth. I said, "First, let me ask you this question, how do you really know you love someone"? He said, "Well, you can be in love with a person or you can be in love with just the things they have to offer to the relationship". I said, "How do you know when you are really in love with a person"? He said, "When you're in love with a person, you hear their voice, or see them, and you get this special feeling inside of you"! Then an alarm went off in me that said, "You're not in love with your husband"! I began to feel that I had sinned big time because I was married but in love with another man!

I said, "Oh Lord, I am in trouble, help me! What am I going to do?" The Lord said, "You did not know that it was still there because it has been covered up for a long time. The other relationships you had been involved in since then have caused this to be suppressed and covered up". He said, "That's why you have not been prospering, because you have not allowed me to deal with the hidden things of the heart".

As I was about to answer him and emergency situation came up with one of the kids and it deter us away from the conversation. The Lord was showing me what I needed to deal with in my heart and He allowed me years later to deal with it. The continuation of that story will be in my next book after the process is completed called "Help Lord! I'm married and have issues in my heart.

I could not believe that for all those years I had been living a lie. I had invited the Lord into my heart but had not allowed Him to dig up the real issues in my life! The Lord has chosen our hearts to dwell in because that is where the real issues of life dwell. He said in Proverbs 4:23, "*Guard your heart with all diligence, out of it flows the issues of life*".

Out of the mouth of babes and nursing infants you have ordained strength because of your enemies."

Psalm 8:2

How Children Suffer in "Unequally Yoked Environments

It was not God's will for my children and me to live in that type of environment. My own disobedience to the Lord, and my husband's addiction caused my children to suffer greatly.

When the time came for my deliverance the Lord spoke to my heart to prepare to move to a new place. While preparing to move to this new place, my husband said that he felt he was not to go with us. When he voiced his decision, it was a confirmation of what I had been feeling.

When I told the kids that he was not going with us they were very happy. They began to gather their belongings and quickly pack in order to leave the bondage they had been living in for so many years. They were beginning to see the light at the end of their tunnel and were moving toward it, but I was still somewhat caught up in the storm clouds. I sensed the storm was beginning to subside but the light seemed very dim to me. We were like the children of Israel when they got ready to leave Egypt.

My husband started attending Alcoholic Anonymous meetings during the time we were waiting for the landlord to get our new place ready. The devil was cleverly using this to distract me to make me think there was a change taking place in his life. He had never reached out for help like that during the years we had been married. He attended a meeting every night until it was time for us to move. His behavior changed tremendously but it was a trick of the devil and I did not recognize it. The day we had to move he offered to help us. After we had completely moved into our new home, he brought his things over and put them in the closet. As soon as he left the kids started screaming, saying, "Mama I know you are not going to let him move in! They were not happy about that at all! I allowed his decision of going go to AA and his new behavior to justify me allowing him to move back in. Seven months later he was back to his old habit. I said, "Lord, what happened"?

That night the Lord gave me a vision. I saw myself breast-feeding an infant. When I woke up I got up and went to my prayer closet to pray. I said, "Lord, what does the dream mean"? He said, read Psalm 8:2, "*Out of the mouth of babes and nursing infants you have ordained strength because of your enemies."* Then the Lord said, "You were not supposed to let him move in. I was trying to tell you through your children but you would not listen".

I began to repent of my disobedience to the Lord and asked Him to deliver me again. At that point I was afraid of what might happen to me because of my disobedience, so I began to yield myself to His mercy. One Sunday my daughter asks me could she go and spend the day with one of her friends. After she left I found a note she had written to me. She said, "Mama, I love you very much, but I left because I could not stay in that situation any longer. There are some things that happened that I am not able to talk about right now, but maybe one day I will. I am tired of having to go through those things, so it's best that I leave. When I found out about the abuse she had been encountering I was shocked, then I understood why she chose to leave. I couldn't speak for a moment but in my heart I said, "Run, baby, run!" because I felt her pain. You can't imagine the pain I felt at that moment. It was like someone took a knife and stabbed my heart.

My children and I were just about to be delivered and I had messed it up. Now here I was dealing with even more pain and devastation. I thought, "Maybe God is punishing me now; He is taking my daughter away from me because of my disobedience to Him." As I began to cry out to the Lord, He spoke these words to me, "Stand still and see the salvation of the Lord"!

I decided to trust God to take care of this situation, and He put it into my sister and brother-in-law's heart to take my daughter into their home. I was so thankful because my sister lived one house over from mine. The Lord put my daughter in a place where I could still see her. When I would see her, from a short distance, my heart would ache but the Lord would reaffirm His Word to me again, "Stand still and see the salvation of the Lord." Those were the words that comforted me during this time. The Lord began the process of deliverance in my life.

One morning, the Lord spoke to my heart to fast and pray for three days concerning my marriage. He said, "On the third day, I will speak to you." As I was contemplating this, the Lord spoke to a special friend of mine to visit me. She said, "The Lord told me to tell you to fast for three days concerning your marriage." I said, "This is truly a confirmation but I have a hard time fasting, and I can't do this on my own." She said, "You have to ask the Lord for His ability to do it". On the third day after fasting and praying I sat quietly before the Lord and listened for Him to speak. He said these words to me, "You are going to get a job and then you are going to separate." As soon as He spoke those words, I got up from prayer because I knew in the spirit it was done. As a matter of fact, I didn't even think about it anymore! When it happened, I knew those were the words God had surely spoken to me.

Two weeks later, it happened just the way the Lord had said. I was hired as Secretary at First Baptist Church, where Rev. J.D. Dupree serves as pastor. This was the church that I attended when I was a young child.

A few weeks later, my husband asked me for a separation. I said, "Lord, what do I do"? The Lord said, "Go to the Word." I went to the Word of God and it fell open to I Corinthians 7:15, "But if the unbelieving departs, let him depart. A brother or sister is not under bondage in such cases, but God hath called us to peace".

Later that afternoon another lady came over to minister to me. She said, "Loretta, I went to a conference in Anaheim, California, to hear Bishop T.D. Jakes". She said, "I know you probably haven't heard of him before, but I brought this audio tape back because it's for you". She said, "The whole time he was preaching, I was thinking about how much you needed to hear this message"!

Around 2:00 a.m. the Lord woke me up and said, "Get up and listen to that tape". The first thing Bishop Jakes said on that tape was, "I came all the way from West Virginia to Anaheim, California to deliver a message to someone". He said, "I'm just a postman, I don't know what you have been going through, or who you been going through it with, but the Lord sent me to tell you that the struggle is over"! He said, "The Lord has broken the chains of the enemy over your life during the night and the Lord wants to serve an eviction notice on your struggle". He said, "Put it out of your house, out of your mind, and out of your emotions'!

The next morning, I woke up feeling as if a load had been lifted off my shoulder. It was then that I realized that the Lord had broken the soul ties and was setting me free! When you've been in a struggle for so long, you may not know how to walk out. You can't do it on your own. God has to bring you out just like He did the children of Israel. They had been in bondage for such a long time until they became familiar with that lifestyle. The Lord had to literally take them by the hand and bring them out. The next day, another lady who had gone to the same conference in Anaheim brought me a video by T.D. Jakes. It was called "A Satisfied Woman." Later that afternoon, as I was doing a few chores of the day, I began to listen to the tape. All of a sudden, the Holy Spirit prompted me to stop doing what I was doing and really listen and when I did, the Holy Spirit began to talk to me through Bishop Jakes. He said, "The reason some people stay in abusive situations is because they think they have no alternative". It seemed like this man was "reading my mail.

I began to think to myself, how am I going to make it on my own?

While I was thinking about this, Bishop Jakes said with a very loud, authoritative voice, "With God on your side, you can do anything! Drag yourself out of that! Come out of that"! As I stood listening to him and hanging on every word, I began to feel a tugging in my heart. Then boldness was deposited in my spirit; I squared my shoulders and began to say, "Yes, with God on my side, I can do anything"!

That same night (on my way to Wednesday night service) I said, "Lord, if you are truly setting me free, let the preacher say these words tonight, 'YOU ARE FREE!'" As the service went on, I completely forgot what I had asked God to do.

The youth pastor was preaching that night and a few minutes after he dismissed the service he interrupted and said out loud, "Hold it for a minute I just want to say these words, HE THAT THE SON SETS FREE IS FREE INDEED! YOU ARE FREE! YOU ARE FREE!" As I was reaching down to get my purse those words resonated in my spirit something burst inside me like a well of joy! Laughter began to spring up within me followed by a river of tears. As soon as this happened, a quick vision flashed before me! I saw myself standing in a prison cell with the door flung wide open. Then I saw the Lord beckoning me to come out. I did not know how to walk out because I was used to being bound. I was bound up in fear; in my mind, will, and emotions. When we have lived in bondage for so long, we don't know what it is to be free! The reason many people can't walk out of bondage is because they are not free inside. Freedom comes from the inside and then out! We have to be free inside to be able to walk it out! Only God can break those chains that are holding us captive inside!

I walked over to the youth pastor, with joy in my heart and tears flowing down my cheeks, and said, "Thank you, Pastor Troy, for obeying the Holy Spirit! I am free"! He and others rejoiced with me because they knew my struggle of thirteen years!

This was the beginning of my deliverance! This was truly the Lord's doing. I knew in my heart that the Lord was setting me free! He said in his Word in John 8:36,

"If the son therefore shall make you free, ye shall be free indeed". Even after the Lord confirmed to me through His Word that I was free, I was still unable to walk out on my own. He literally had to take me by the hand and lead me out in order for me to receive the promise that he had for me.

After my husband asked me for a separation, the Lord had to lead me step by step. First, He began ministering to me about soul ties. He said, "I want you to stop having sexual relations with this man because I have broken the soul tie between the two of you"! He said, "If you keep sleeping with him, you will have then allowed your soul to be joined back to his soul". Two people do not become one by saying;" I do" to each other. This happens through sexual bonding. This is what creates soul ties in intimate exchanges.

The day I received my separation papers was on the anniversary date of my marriage. The Lord said to me, "I cut it off the very date that you put it together, so you would know this was my doing"!

He brought me out and he brought my daughter back home to live with me again. When He brings you forth, He always brings you forth with peace. He said in Isaiah 55:12, "*You shall go out with joy and be led forth with peace.*" He gave me a supernatural peace as He walked me through the process.

A Miracle in the Process

One day at work I began feeling sorry for myself while meditating on the failure of my marriage and all of the things I had been through. Out of frustration, I began to yell out to the Lord, saying, "Okay, show me what else is in my heart! What do you want with me?" At that very moment, I wasn't sure what God was after.

After I settled down, and began to get quiet, the Lord began to speak to me. He said, "Your daughter's dad is going to call you." When He spoke those words to me, joy began welling up in my heart! Two years had passed since that first phone call after eighteen years. The phone rang immediately after the Lord spoke those words to my heart. To my surprise it was just as the Lord had spoken. It was he. I said, "You are not going to believe this". He said, "I already know! God told me to call you"! Tears began rolling down my face, and joy sprang up in my heart. He was so thrilled that he had finally found me to connect with his daughter! He greatly anticipated seeing his daughter! This was perfect timing and it was the Lord's doing! He asked to fly my daughter to Virginia, to a family reunion so that all of his family could meet her for the first time. This brought joy to my heart as well. I began to think, "Since God showed me two years ago that he was the man that I really loved, maybe God is bringing this reunion around for me as well'. Little did I know but it was only part of the process that I had to go through.

When I began seeking the Lord considering my going to Virginia, He spoke to my heart and said, "Not now! You are not ready". He said, "this is not your time this is your daughter and her dad's time'. To my surprise, it was truly the Lord's doing and not mines! I was going through a hard time at this moment and just wanted some happiness to cling to. As the tears begin to roll down my face I could feel the Lord's hand catch each one. His presence was so tangible I could actually feel Him holding me and assuring me that He was going to see me through all of this. This was a very happy moment for my daughter when she was able to see her father for the first time. The Lord had answered her prayer that one day she would find her daddy. The Word says that, "He will turn the hearts of the fathers back to their children, and the children to the fathers"

(Malachi 4:6). God had a plan and He was working it for our good. "And we know that all things work together for good to them that love God, to them who are the called according to his purpose" (Romans 8:28). He said that all things "work together" for good, not that the thing you are encountering will be the final answer. The thing is part of the process that is working together with something else that will usher in God's purpose. That's why we have to trust God and not our own way. "A man's heart plans his way but the Lord direct his steps" (Proverbs 16:9).

The Lord had not only given him his daughter back but (five year later) a new granddaughter!

When You Are Free Then You Can Fly

I had lived in bondage to a sin and in its subsequent pain for thirteen years! But the Lord was faithful to bring me out, and untangle me from the snares that Satan used to bind me. I can truly say that God is a God of deliverance. No one can deliver you like He can—if you trust Him to do it.

The Lord wrought a great deliverance in my life and now I am able to "fly again." He released me from unhealthy restraints and placed healthy boundaries in my life. I now can fly to greater heights with the Lord's Harness about me. After I got a taste of freedom after being bound for so long I literally would feel exhausted. I said, "Lord, "Will I ever settle down?" He said, "What does a bird do when he is locked up in a cage, and one day the door opens"? I said, "He flies everywhere"! The Lord said, "You are like that little bird in that cage. You were once a prisoner inside and I have opened the door. You are now experiencing the freedom to fly, but now with my harness about you because you have submitted to the Master's will for your life".

My next orders from the Lord were to move to

Dallas, Texas. I was somewhat afraid because I had never left my Louisiana hometown. Leaving a small town and moving to a big city was very intimidating for me.

As I began to drag my feet on this decision, the brooks began to dry up, and all provision seemed to diminish. My daughter said, "Mama, what do you have to lose? Maybe the Lord has plans for you in Texas and He has allowed your provision to dry up here so you would move forward." At that moment, I felt such a peace come over me. The next morning the Lord woke me up around 3:00 a.m. and said, "Get up. I want to talk to you." I got up, went sat on the front porch and began to pray and wait on the Lord. I said, "Lord, why does Texas, keep coming up in my spirit?" He said, "What do you keep talking about all the time?" I said, "I keep talking about moving to Texas." He said, "You keep talking about it because I put it in your heart, and out of the abundance of the heart the mouth speaketh"!

Immediately, the wrestling in my heart began to cease. I knew that the Lord was leading me and that

He had a plan for my life. He assured me that He was going to be with me wherever he leads. So I packed two suitcases, and set out on a journey, not knowing what the Lord had in store for me!

God's Faithfulness

It had been twelve years since I had move from Louisiana to Dallas, Texas. My life changed tremendously when I took that step of obedience to the Lord. It seemed like I had stepped into the promise land of milk and honey. God open up so many doors of opportunities for me. I meet new people of all cultures of different languages. God took my life to a new level in Him.

One beautiful sunny day as I was waking up to get ready for work I received a phone call from my sister in-law saying that my ex-husband was in the hospital seriously ill. She said, "The reason I am calling you is because I remembered a dream that you told me about years ago how the Lord had showed you that He was going to save him. The doctors said that he has cirrhosis of the liver and his kidney has stopped functioning properly and there was nothing they could do for him but make him comfortable. I remember your faithfulness of praying for him all those years you were married to him". I said, excitedly, "Yes the Lord told me that He was going to save him." She added, "Can I give you the number to the hospital where he is and maybe you can pray with him. I said, "I will be honored to do that because the Lord wishes that no one would perish but all would come to repentance".

When I called he answered he answered in a very weak voice tone voice. When I begin to talk with him I lost the connections and the prompted me to call right back. The Lord said, "Get right to the point quickly." I said, "Lee, do you know Jesus"? He asked, "who'? I answered, "Jesus." He responded, Oh, yes I know him. He said it as if I was talking about and old friend of his that lived down the street. I asked him, "Are you ready to ask Jesus into your heart? You know, I always told you that the Lord was going to save you". He said, "Yes that's true, I'm ready". I lead him through the sinners' prayer and he accepted the Lord as his personal savior. Immediately after we got through praying, he said with an upbeat tone, "I feel good now!" I said with excitement, "I know that you do". Then I said to him, "Oh! By the way if you get to Heaven before I do you tell Jesus I love Him with all my heart". He said with excitement, "I'm going to do that. I said, "God bless you Lee". He said with a very thankful voice. "God bless you, too". I called my sister-in-law back and told her that he had accepted the Lord as his personal savior. She said, the Lord told me to get you to pray for Lee". Three days later around 5:00 am she called me and told me that he had passed and went home to be with the Lord. After I hung the phone up I sat up in the bed and said to the Lord, "Lord, you are something else, after all these years of him and I being divorced you used me to lead him to you.

The Lord said to me, "I told you I was going to save him at the end of his life and I used you so you would know that I fulfilled the promise'! I said, "Lord you are truly faithful"!! He said, "Now that the promise is fulfilled write it in your book! At that moment then I realized that "The promise had been fulfilled" and the book was now completed!

A Quote from the Author

Many people give up during the struggle because they don't have an anchor. Jesus is truly our anchor that controls the storms in our life. When we seek Him during the storm He gives us another anchor call hope. That hope is a personal promise straight from the heart of God. If you hold onto the promise and don't jump ship in the mist of the storm, then you will see the faithfulness of God. You might not know when the answer is coming, but you can know that it will."

Loretta Davis

If you would like to contact Ms. Loretta Davis for speaking engagements or to order her books, please use the contact information below.

Ms. Loretta Davis
1717 McKinney Avenue Suite 700
Dallas, Texas 75202
Office: 877-441-7952

Other Books Published by
Loretta Davis

Krazy Dum Stupid Faith Gets Results

Learning to Forgive God's Way

Barnes & Nobles

Amazon.com

Newlifepublishing.us

Made in the USA
Columbia, SC
13 February 2024

31432627R00067